An Expression of LOVE

*Let's Change The World
One Hug At A Time!*

CYNTHIA M. JACKSON

WestBow Press books may be ordered through booksellers or by contacting:

WestBow Press
A Division of Thomas Nelson & Zondervan
1663 Liberty Drive
Bloomington, IN 47403
www.westbowpress.com
844-714-3454

ISBN: 978-1-6642-4620-1 (sc)
ISBN: 978-1-6642-4622-5 (hc)
ISBN: 978-1-6642-4621-8 (e)

Library of Congress Control Number: 2021920309

Print information available on the last page.

WestBow Press rev. date: 10/26/2021

WESTBOW
PRESS®
A DIVISION OF THOMAS NELSON
& ZONDERVAN

Hello, my name is
_____ and I like hugs!

Place or draw a picture of yourself in the space below.

I like hugs when I am happy!
I like hugs when I am sad!
I like hugs even more when I am mad!

My mommy's name is _____.
I hug her every day, so she knows
that I love her very much.

My daddy's name is _____.
I hug him when he comes home from work
because I love him very much, too.

Place or draw a picture of your mommy
and daddy in the space below:

I have a sister named

_____

and a brother named

_____.

I hug my sister and brother because they NEED
hugs too even if they think hugs are not cool.

Place or draw a picture of your sister
and brother in the space below.

I have a pet named _____. I make sure
I hug my pet too, but not too tight. My pet's nose
maybe cold, but it has a very warm heart.

Place or draw a picture of your pet in the space below:

And, I have grandfathers, grandmothers, uncles, aunts, and friends that I do not see very much; but, when I do see them, I hug them, too. They need hugs too! Would you agree?

Place or draw a picture of your family
members and friends in the space below.

Ooh, so many hugs! They make me feel so happy and warm inside even on a cold and rainy day!

Draw a picture of a rainy day in the space below.

When I am not feeling well, I will ask my mommy and daddy for a hug. Sometimes they are so busy, they may not even know that I need a hug.

Draw a picture of yourself when you are
not feeling well in the space below.

I am careful not to hug a stranger especially if mommy and daddy are not around-that is for sure. If anyone tries to hurt me or give me candy or toys, I will run to tell mommy and daddy.

Draw a picture of what you think a stranger
looks like in the space below.

Hugs are nice and free. They are powerful too. Hugs help us show our love for our family members and friends. Hugs will change a sad face to a happy face. Hugs just make our days much brighter.

Draw a picture of what you think a happy
day looks like in the space below.

So, the next time mommy, daddy, sister, or brother
seems to be having a bad day or even a good day,
make it a better day by giving them a GREAT
BIG BEAR HUG! It will make YOU smile TOO!

Draw a picture of what you think a happier
world would look like in the space below.

All Right Hugs

Hugs in the morning
hugs at night
sometimes short OR sometimes long,
no matter when
we can't go wrong!

Hugs in the morning
hugs at night
sometimes simple OR sometimes tight,
no matter how
they're always just right!

-Cynthia M. Jackson

About the Author

She is the mother of three beautiful daughters who taught her how to hug and verbally say "I love you". She grew up in a very close knit family. Even though she did not hear those endearing words much while growing up or experience many hugs, she always KNEW she was loved. She genuinely loves people and wants everyone to experience love, even if it begins with only a simple hug.

Printed in the United States
by Baker & Taylor Publisher Services